A Flower Of The Field: Eliza's Song And The
Five Refrains Following

Henry Nehemiah Dodge

In the interest of creating a more extensive selection of rare historical book reprints, we have chosen to reproduce this title even though it may possibly have occasional imperfections such as missing and blurred pages, missing text, poor pictures, markings, dark backgrounds and other reproduction issues beyond our control. Because this work is culturally important, we have made it available as a part of our commitment to protecting, preserving and promoting the world's literature. Thank you for your understanding.

A FLOWER OF THE FIELD

BY
HENRY NEHEMIAH DODGE

READ BY
Rev. FREDERICK A. BISBEE, S.T.D.
AT THE DEDICATION OF THE OLD POTTER HOUSE AT GOOD
LUCK, N. J., AUGUST 16TH, 1914

ELIZA'S SONG

AND THE FIVE REFRAINS FOLLOWING

SUNG BY
Mrs. WILLIAM HENRY McGLAUFLIN

PUBLISHED BY THE MURRAY PRESS
FOR THE MURRAY GROVE ASSOCIATION
1914

COPYRIGHT, 1914
BY
HENRY NEHEMIAH DODGE

HENRY NEHEMIAH DODGE

OLD POTTER DWELLING HOUSE,
GOOD LUCK, N.J.

INTRODUCTION

BY THE REV. FREDERICK A. BISBEE, S. T. D.

A FLOWER OF THE FIELD

A valuable contribution to literature, and to our literature, is made in the poem of Dr. Henry Nehemiah Dodge, which was written for the dedication of the restored Potter House at Good Luck, N. J. Dr. Dodge is one of the very few poets able to sustain strength and interest through a long poem, and in his "Christus Victor" and "John Murray's Landfall" he has given to the world, and the world has appreciatively accepted, two poems which will hold a permanent place in literature. This new work is much shorter, and is an "occasional poem," which of necessity localizes it, but, like some of Whittier's "occasional poems," which rank among his noblest and best efforts, we are convinced that this one from Dr. Dodge has the historic and the literary value which assures it a permanent place. As a part of the literature of Universalism, not only does it make a peculiar and winning appeal to those who have been in sympathetic touch with the sacred memories of Good Luck, but to all who, appreciating the priceless possession of our faith, are some time to seek its sources

INTRODUCTION

and gather new strength as they drink therefrom, the guidance of the wise hand of Dr. Dodge along the historic paths which he has made beautiful with the magic of his verse, will be most welcome.

THE DEDICATION

The story of the dedication of the restored Potter House is of interest in this connection. It was a glorious day. Every one who sensed the significance of this historic place desired to be there to witness the reconsecration of the home of Thomas Potter, in which he entertained John Murray. And it was a happy company which came to the sacred spot on that beautiful Sunday afternoon, August 16, 1914, to participate in the services.

Those who had known the old house set in its tangle of neglected fields, and fast going to ruin, would never recognize the restored building and grounds; but Thomas Potter would have! For while the transformation has been complete, loving and sympathetic spirits have protected the place from being modernized out of its historic significance.

Too much praise can not be given to the Rev. J. L. Wolbach, the resident superintendent, who, with his family, coming to the place late in the spring, with the most meager facilities, had wrought the miracle of change. Mr. John W. Moore of New York, representing the board of trustees, had full

POTTER DWELLING HOUSE RESTORED

charge of the restoration of the building, and Miss Ida R. East, the secretary, was not only the wise guide and counselor, but the hard worker in securing and placing the remarkable collection of magnificent furniture which so befits the surroundings.

Approaching the house from the old church, along the very path over which Murray walked in his first approach, the dignified old building in its rich brown appeals to the highest sentiments. Through the old half-doors we entered the room and stood before the great fireplace, impressed by the sacred memories; we passed up the stairs, which curve right up over the fireplace, to enter the sleeping-chamber, in which Murray did not sleep the first night, but there wrestled with the Lord until the dawn, and there finally came to his decision to deliver the message which was the beginning of the Universalist Church in America.

These rooms, together with the others in the old mansion, have been furnished by generous hands in a most fitting way; there is nothing inharmonious. Hardly a piece of furniture in the place is less than a century old, and the new has been made to conform to the old. These rare pieces have here been gathered as a tribute to the "Herald of Love" and the "Apostle of Faith." To Dr. Henry Nehemiah Dodge, the poet laureate of our faith, and Mrs. Dodge, an especial debt of gratitude is due for their generous and always

INTRODUCTION

fitting contributions. Naturally to them belonged the honor of furnishing John Murray's room. But they did not stop there, but touched with their generous sympathetic taste other points. The Rev. Dr. Marion Crosley, one of our oldest clergymen, had the honor of being one of the first contributors. The Universalist Church in Muncie, Ind., under the leadership of Dr. Edward G. Mason, gave most generously, as did Mrs. Cooper of New York, and many others, so that to-day the Potter House is furnished and made habitable.

The building was crowded to the limit for the services of dedication, which had been carefully arranged by the Rev. W. H. Skeels and Dr. Dodge, and were in charge of the new president of the Murray Grove Association, the Rev. Dr. W. H. McGlauflin.

After the singing, by all present, of Dr. Ballou's hymn, "In God's Eternity," the invocation was offered by the Rev. Emma E. Bailey, who has been one of the most faithful and generous friends of the place, and whose spiritual sympathies knit her close to the house and its associations. Dr. McGlauflin gave a brief address, in which he set certain great historic dates and names, and then the whole company united with him in the following service:

Minister—To religious tolerance and freedom of speech, which gave to all denominations the right of use of the Potter Meeting-house,

INTRODUCTION

People—We dedicate this house.

Minister—To the promulgation of the Gospel of Jesus Christ proclaimed throughout the world down long ages by his disciples and followers as moved by his divine Spirit,

People—We dedicate this house.

Minister—To brotherhood among men and peace among nations, as exemplified in the lives of John Murray and Thomas Potter, and to the firm conviction that men will yet learn that peace is better than war, that love is stronger than hate, and that God's goodness will finally be triumphant,

People—We dedicate this house.

Minister—To the eternal hope voiced by this prophet and this preacher of universal salvation, who met here for the first time, and out of whose meeting came forth the light of religious liberty as the dawn follows the darkest night,

People—We dedicate this house.

Minister—To faith in the possibilities of the future, and to courage to pursue these possibilities to the realization of their highest and holiest ends,

People—We dedicate this house.

Minister—To a sacred belief expressed in the building of a house of God here in the wilderness, that if we sow, He will send the increase, and to a determination to hold this ever in mind through the passing years, so that while individuals may come and go, the cause may finally triumph over all,

People—We dedicate this house.

Minister—To love, which suffereth long and is kind, which envieth not, which vaunteth not itself and is not puffed up, but which beareth all things, believeth all things, hopeth all things, and endureth all things,

Minister and People—We dedicate this house.

INTRODUCTION

The prayer of dedication was offered by the Rev. W. H. Skeels, and it lifted all into an atmosphere favorable to the appreciation of the great event of the day, the delivery of the poem which Dr. Dodge had written for the occasion. The reading of this poem was by the Rev. Dr. Frederick A. Bisbee, and the singing of the introductory song, the refrain introduced along the way, and the concluding song, fortunately fell to the lot of Mrs. W. H. McGlauflin, who with her soulful voice gave rare interpretation. The benediction was pronounced by the Rev. James D. Herrick, of Towanda, Pa.

THE POEM

"A Flower of the Field" tells anew the miracle-story of the awakening of the soul of John Murray from the murk and gloom of a cheerless and oppressive theology, and experiences which cast a black shadow over his life, to the light and glory and inspiration of the universal love and purpose of God.

Through the story runs the refrain, the "Song of Eliza," the young wife who shared with her husband the shadows and the revelation of the light.

Those familiar with the fine work of Dr. Dodge in his poem, "John Murray's Landfall," will recall the historic incidents here given a new setting. The theological gloom of that period through which broke a ray of light in the larger vision of James Relly, the hiding in that dark soil of the little "seed of thought that lives to-day," caught the imagination of John Murray and his young wife, made them glad in the message they were to deliver, and as he preached, she sang of the unfolding flower which could not die.

But even as the vision stirred their hearts, death lifted high his pitiless dart and smote their first-born son, and soon laid upon the shoulders of the preacher the still heavier cross, as the wife of his young manhood drooped and died, and in disheartening solitude he faced a world of cruel misunderstanding and bitter enmity, from which he fled to hide himself in the wilderness of the New World.

But while bowed in discouragement over the disasters of his life, and fleeing from a seemingly relentless fate, the seed of the "Little Flower, trodden under foot, crushed by the heel of wrong," had taken root in another heart, and when the fleeing "Herald of Love" touched the shore of the New World, he was met by the "Apostle of Faith," who commanded him to speak.

Then began the struggle between John Murray and Thomas Potter, between Murray and himself, and with his God, through the long hours of the night in the chamber of the old mansion, until the soul of the preacher surrendered, and in the little church which the "Apostle of Faith" had built with his own hands, the "Herald of Love" proclaimed his message, which was to reshape the religious thinking of the world.

The Little Flower of the Field new-set in the garden of God's humanity, its fragrance is to encircle the world.

A FLOWER OF THE FIELD

A Flower of the Field.
Words by Henry Nehemiah Dodge
Melodie Belmont
by Samuel Webbe
Lit – tle Flower, – lit – tle Flower, Thy
breath is waft – ed wide, — The murk and gloom have
felt thy power, And may not long a – bide

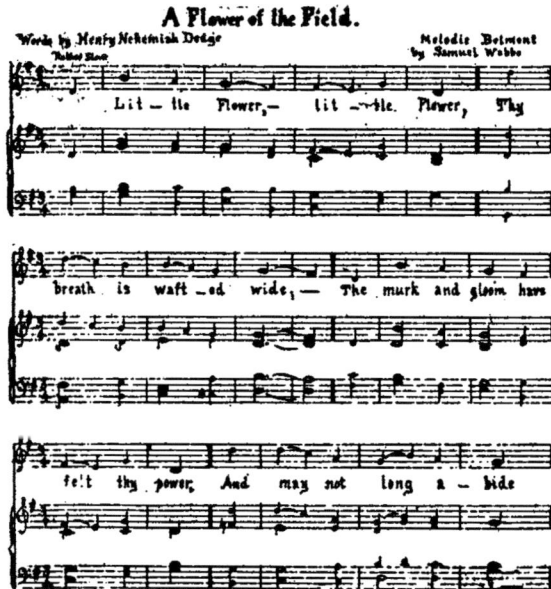

A FLOWER OF THE FIELD

(To be Sung)

"Frowning forests hid the sun,
* The sun that shines for all;*
The path of Hope, in light begun,
* Lay buried 'neath a pall.*

"Beneath the snow a floweret sweet
* Was dreaming of the day*
When Springtide light its bloom should greet
* With long-forgotten ray.*

"Hope, scenting fragrance in the gloom,
* Pressed on with hastening wing—*
Of this sweet blossom's heartening bloom
* My gladdened soul would sing.*

"Little Flower, little Flower,
* Thy breath is wafted wide;*
The murk and gloom have felt thy power,
* And may not long abide."*

A FLOWER OF THE FIELD

Adown the years, from long ago,
  Soft sings Eliza's voice;
Afar I hear the rapture flow,
  And with her song rejoice.

Her soul deliverance had found
  From terrors of the past;
Saw Love supreme o'er sin abound,
  Victorious at last.

Rejoicing with her song, I say,
  The gloom is fleeing far;
Winter is melting into May,
  And risen the Morning Star!

For ages long night hid the sun
  In medieval gloom;
The path of Hope, in light begun,
  Led to eternal doom.

Eternal doom, eternal doom,
  Tolling for Liberty;
Eternal doom, Hope's rayless tomb,
  Keystone of tyranny!

A FLOWER OF THE FIELD

What demon-council forged this brand
   Fair Liberty to slay;
Prelate and monarch hand in hand,
   Lords of the Judgment Day?

O precious Flower, O precious Flower,
   Thy seed lay buried long;
Trod by the haughty sons of power,
   Crushed by the heel of Wrong!

A thousand years crept slowly by;
   Thy rootlets darkling slept;
To Heaven oft rose the martyr's cry;
   Full oft thy children wept.

Then rose the waking sun, and day
   Streamed on the startled night;
The fading phantoms flee away
   Before the oncoming light.

   (To be Sung)
O Light of Love, O sacred Flower,
   Thy breath is wafted wide;
The murk and gloom have felt thy power,
   And may not long abide.

And may not long abide, for lo!
  Almighty Love doth reign;
The eternal stream doth onward flow,
  Nor shall it flow in vain.

* *

Undaunted of the gloom a soul,
  A mighty soul, arose;
Love's Herald saw the hurt made whole—
  Love conquering all His foes.

In "Union" saw he all our race
  Inseverably one;
Hid in the ample Heart of Grace,
  The heart of Calvary's Son.

On that stupendous day of woe
  Love hid us in His heart;
Love would not let the sinner go,
  Nor from the vilest part.

Justice demanded penalty,
  Atonement for our sin;
Love purchased us and set us free
  Or ever we had been.

A FLOWER OF THE FIELD

He saw no other God above,
  He saw no man below;
Christ was the very Heart of Love,
  Whose glory he would show.

In God he saw no longer three
  Divinities in one;
He worshiped *Perfect Unity*,
  Of God and Man the Son.

'Twas but symbolic imagery!
  Yea, our most precious thought,
Where Justice one with Love we see,
  Love's Herald darkly sought.

These ancient symbols voice the need
  Love knows Himself to give;
Love's Passion, told in rite and creed—
  Through sacrifice to live.

In his crude system hid the seed
  Of thought that lives to-day;
Truth that a hungering world shall feed,
  With ever widening sway.*

---
* See Appendix.

A FLOWER OF THE FIELD

And we, perchance, as dimly see
  What yet doth wait in store
Of Truth's august infinity,
  Disclosing more and more,

As time flows on, the vast design
  Of Man's inheritance:
The wondrous thought of Love Divine
  Our glory to enhance.

He turned our faces toward the light,
  Amid the engulfing gloom—
Though we may see with clearer sight,
  A giant doth he loom.

What though he conquered Pisgah's height
  By ways we do not tread?
He scaled the steep whose growing light
  Now streams upon our head!

He saw our sundered, sin-hurt race
  United and complete;
Clasped in Almighty Love's embrace,
  Drawn by Compassion Sweet.

A FLOWER OF THE FIELD

He saw our manhood lifted high,
    Made Godlike on the Cross;
Clothed on with immortality,
    Redeemed from sin and loss.

No more was Heaven a citadel
    For trembling refugees
Snatched from the ravening jaws of Hell,
    A Despot's whim to please.

Heaven was the vast, o'erarching dome
    Beyond all time and space;
Of every man the ancestral home,
    Lit by the Father's face,

Where should be healed each broken tie,
    Failure with victory crowned,
Joy everlasting fill the sky,
    And life, more life abound.

O Sea of Sovereign Love Divine,
    Unfathomed Sympathy,
The world's vast stress and pain were Thine,
    Majestic Unity!

A FLOWER OF THE FIELD

Around Thy throne all worlds revolved,
    All souls were knit to Thee,
Sin's minor chord by love resolved—
    Eternal Symphony!

Inwove through all a golden thread,
    Thrown by a Hand Divine,
Wrought for the living and the dead
    Love's marvelous design.

Thou gav'st the joy of morning glow,
    The splendor of high noon,
The twilight shadows moving slow,
    And slumber's nightly boon.

Thou gav'st the Spring's sweet roundelay,
    The Summer's golden dream,
Autumn enrobed in proud array,
    Snow-wreath and frozen stream.

'Twas Love that brimmed the mighty deep,
    That built the mountains high;
'Twas Love whose tempests headlong sweep
    Athwart the flaming sky;

A FLOWER OF THE FIELD

Whose silent constellations march
   Adown the starry vast,
The Galaxy's resplendent arch,
   With diamonds over-cast.

Thou, Love, art Master of all time,
& Lord thou of Man's career:
Of birth, of death, peace, war's dread crime,
   Joy, pestilence and fear.

Thou art the Life, the Soul, the Core
   Of the vast universe—
Love's Herald ceased, he could no more,
   Love's message to rehearse.

(To be Sung)
Little Flower, little Flower,
   Thy breath is wafted wide;
The murk and gloom have felt thy power,
   And may not long abide.

       *   *

Lo! as the vision stirred his heart—
   Heaven's rapture here begun—
Death lifted high his pitiless dart
   And smote his firstborn son.

A FLOWER OF THE FIELD

The future reeled before the blow,
   As fell the father's tears;
The mother knelt in silent woe,
   Mourning the sunless years.

The lily that beside him bloomed,
   And sweet her fragrance shed,
She, too, by the Destroyer doomed,
   Drooping, erelong was dead.

Alas, ah me! his love lay dead.
   His soul, with anguish torn,
Bowed low. Soon on his storm-beat head
   Rained lurid shafts of scorn.

Branded as heretic, outcast
   From the circle of the elect,
His soul into the darkness passed,
   His life in shame was wrecked.

For him who doth the light proclaim
   Which night-birds cannot see,
The fowls of darkness will defame,
   And smirch with calumny.

A FLOWER OF THE FIELD

O broken heart, O grieving soul,
    Love's mystery moved in thee;
Thy sorrows wrought to make us whole,
    To give us liberty!

O'er ocean-seas Love's Herald fled,
    From grief to find surcease;
The past is done, the future dead—
    Come solitude of peace!

Breathe on his spirit, Ocean Wind,
    Breathe on him, Ocean Calm;
Breathe on his spirit till he find
    Thy breath a healing balm!

* *

Lo! on yon looming strand I see
    A mighty man of God,
Bronzed by the winds of land and sea,
    A tiller of the sod.

A toiler of the sea and land,
    A soul to do and dare,
Wrought he for Love, with toil-scarred hand,
    To build his vision fair.

For he had seen, with wondering eye,
  The Dayspring from afar;
The lighting of the Eastern sky;
  The Victor's flashing car.

Upon his darkness faintly shone
  The Fullness of the Lord—
How shall our coldness e'er atone
  The light we have ignored?

And in that house the Lord would show
  What he had dimly seen—
Rejoice, O sea, rejoicing flow;
  Rejoice, ye pastures green!

As long he wrought from day to day,
  Fanned by the sea's sweet breath,
His heart was seeking far away
  A home in Nazareth.

A Prophet of heroic mould,
  A Man of Faith was he,
Whose valiant soul on Truth took hold
  With no uncertainty.

A FLOWER OF THE FIELD

Eyes had he kindred to the light,
  Where others blindly grope;
The vision grasped his piercing sight,
  Where others faintly hope.

Nor waited he another's word
  To build his vision fair;
Unto the task his loins to gird,
  Nor cringed he to Despair.

Alone he reared Love's new abode;
  Joy rang in every blow—
'Tis weakling Fear that needs the goad;
  How slow our hearts, how slow!

* *

Unto his soul the Spirit spoke:
  "Thy joy is now at hand;
My chosen vessel, tempest-broke,
  Is mooring on yon strand.

"Locked in his breast my precious word
  Thy hand shall free again;
Thou, who the still, small Voice hast heard,
  Shalt give this boon to men."

A FLOWER OF THE FIELD

(To be Sung)
Little Flower, little Flower!
　Thy breath is wafted wide;
The murk and gloom have felt thy power,
　And may not long abide.

　　　　* *

The wanderer came, he sought the wild
　To hide his sorrow there.
The Prophet met Love's wayward child,
　And conquered his despair.

As when the battle turns to rout,
　And Panic flees the field;
Nor threat, nor blow, nor thundered shout
　From dire destruction shield,

Sudden the clang of hooves is heard;
　A foaming steed appears,
And, godlike, to a fiery word
　Panic gives way with cheers,

So did the Prophet's stern command
　Arrest the fugitive,
And, with his Heaven-invoking hand,
　Bid him *arise and live.*

A FLOWER OF THE FIELD

These leafy shades did whisper then;
  Joy filled each forest glade,
And, breathing low, yon salty fen
  Antiphonal flute-notes made.

The sea that bare him to our shore
  A mighty anthem raised;
With solemn chant shall evermore
  Almighty Love be praised.

* *

Sing, worshiping, O Sacred Muse,
  The wondrous mystery:
How oft the weak things God doth choose
  To show His majesty!

With foolish things He doth confound
  The wise in their conceit—
A little child the way hath found
  Unto His mercy seat.

  (To be Sung)
Little Flower, little Flower!
  Thy breath is wafted wide;
The murk and gloom have felt thy power,
  And may not long abide.

A FLOWER OF THE FIELD

Age-long the night of terror gloomed
  Upon the Church of God,
Till sweet this Heavenly Floweret bloomed,
  Sprung from the wintry sod.

The night-wrack hid the Father's face—
  The human heart a slave—
Tyranny crushed a fear-swept race;
  Who shall the people save?

O Son of Man, upon Thy heart
  This Floweret ever bear;
It cannot live from Thee apart;
  Let it Thy travail share!

O Son of God, enthroned on high,
  Triumphant over death—
This sacred Flower shall fill the Sky
  With fragrance of its breath.

* *

Ye pilgrims from afar, behold
  This roof-tree, bent with years,
Where Love met Faith in days of old;
  Where Doubt forgot his fears.

A FLOWER OF THE FIELD

Faith to this hearthstone welcomed Love;
   This threshold felt their tread;
Here angels, hastening from above,
   Unto the conflict sped.

Here, wrestling with self-will all night,
   Love's Herald overcame,
And won for us the mortal fight—
   All honor to his name!

Tread softly in this hallowed shrine
   Which now we dedicate
To Faith, to Love of Truth Divine—
   Forever consecrate.

Nor clustering spire, nor swelling dome,
   Nor stately pillared nave
More hallowed than Love's ancient home
   Beside the sun-lit wave.

* *

When the lone beacon kindled here
   Hath shed its beams afar,
Grown in the decades drawing near
   Unto a burning star;

A FLOWER OF THE FIELD

(Guard well this beacon's holy fire,
  Let not its flame decline;
Add precious fuel! Fiercer, higher
  Leap forth its light divine!)

When in the flood of lapsing years
  The Church, with clearer sight,
Shall banish medieval fears,
  And greet the rising light,

Hither, impelled by Love's behest,
  A multitude shall flow
From every shrine, in sacred quest,
  Glad homage here to show

Unto our sires who steadfast stood,
  Their banner on the wind,
Blazoned in light: *God's Fatherhood
The utmost soul shall find.*

Not theirs alone their gallant fight,
  Their tears, their martyrdom:
Toiled they, lone heroes of the light,
  To free the Church to come.

A FLOWER OF THE FIELD

Those sun-lit folds through seven score years
    Have flown, to cheer the world
Through all the strife, the blood, the tears,
    Nor shall they e'er be furled!

Think not the age-long fight is won—
    Nay, Christian, arm thee well!—
A vaster, deadlier strife is on,
    With the dread powers of Hell.

Oncoming see their cohorts loom
    Implacable as death!
They drown the sun in ancient gloom,
    They poison with their breath.

Nor age nor sex is spared by Greed—
    World-wide the bitter cry!—
Privilege has not changed its creed,
    Chanting Convention's lie.

These follow close a monstrous brood,
    Born of dim-waking thought;
Strange counterfeits of Brotherhood,
    By ancient ills distraught.

Smoulder inquisitorial fires
  Of bigotry; fierce hate
Of race for race with war conspires
  The earth to desolate;

The mystery of Orient,
  The Equatorial night—
These all plead that our strength be lent;
  Plead for our greater light.

Come, Spirit of Divine Accord,
  And draw all hearts to Thee
Till every tongue shall own Thee Lord—
  Come in Thy majesty!

* *

The winds of God—oh, portent strange!—
  Courage, devoted band!—
The winds of God *"will never change,"*
  Till Truth o'erflow the land.

To Barnegat they urge the tide,
  The billows hither roll;
Hither they surge from far and wide—
  Rejoice, my waiting soul!

A FLOWER OF THE FIELD

(To be Sung)

Little Flower, little Flower,
  Who breath'st on hill and mead,
Lo, here we sing, in this glad hour,
  The planting of thy seed!

The sowing of the seed we know,
  The full bloom Earth shall see,
The fruitage Heaven alone may show
  Through blest eternity.

APPENDIX

For the story of "Eliza" see "John Murray's Landfall," pp. 72-104.

That Murray, as well as other theologians of the past—framers of the ancient creeds and formulas—"darkly sought" "our most precious thought" would appear from the extracts quoted below. The idea that Christ gave himself as a sacrifice for the sins of mankind, to satisfy the justice of God, and that God and Christ are *one*, is but a crude way of saying, through symbolic imagery, what we now rejoice in believing, namely, *that the love and justice of God are one and the same thing.*

In a sense, this thought, unconsciously held, explains, in some degree, the tenacity with which the doctrines of the Trinity and the Atonement have been held throughout Christendom for many ages.

To the multitude concrete symbolism makes a stronger appeal than logic. The human heart loves poetry, and is not afraid of paradox, and when the new theology ripens into poetic form it will take a stronger hold upon the popular heart.

To the mind of the Universalist, there need be no essential conflict between the systems of Murray and Ballou, if we remember that one preceded the other, and that they were both feeling after the same One God. Like many others before them, neither succeeded fully in expressing that which is ineffable.

We read in Murray's Letters and Sketches:

"Awake for me the judgment thou hast commanded. Ps. vii. Dear precious Lamb of God! How much was thy heart set on giving glory to the Highest, and, by so doing, establishing peace on earth and good will to men. So ardently did our Emmanuel desire this judgment, that, although certain it would cause the sweat as great drops of blood to issue from every distended pore of his agonized body, yet his heart, made up of tenderness and love for the people he was to purchase, engaged to approach before God in the judgment He had commanded." Vol. I, p. 267.

"Let us not only look, but let us keep our eye steadfastly fixed on this soul-satisfying sight; let us look until every other consideration is swallowed up in holy veneration of a spectacle so mysterious, so divine; until we feel every faculty expanded and filled with unbounded love to this Lamb of God who taketh away the sin of the world; until we are constrained to exclaim: Thou art worthy of the kingdom, the power, and the glory, for thou wast slain, and hast redeemed us to God by thy blood." Vol. I, p. 186.

"The creature can never fall lower than the lowest. Jesus Christ was made in the likeness of sinful flesh; he was the highest and the lowest. There was no God above him, nor no man beneath him. I am, said Emmanuel, the Alpha and Omega. He is the foundation and the top-stone. And in his character will be made manifest in presence of every creature in heaven, on earth, and in the sea, that perfect righteousness, which, as a garment, shall cover *every member of that mystical body of which he is the ever perfect, ever dignified, ever glorious head.* And the day which approaches will reveal the salvation of the complete piece, of the whole family of man, when the whole human nature, having one new heart, shall, from the fullness of this new heart, ascribe to the world's Saviour all might, majesty, power, and dominion, worlds without end. Amen and Amen." Vol. III, p. 325.

". . . As I believe Jesus Christ to be the only wise God our Saviour, I know no other God in whom to trust, or of whom to be afraid. I am a Unitarian. I believe in one God over all blessed forever, and I am persuaded that it is this one God who is the Saviour of all men. The fullness of the Deity, I conceive, dwelt bodily in the humanity, and I believe that he himself spoke by the prophets, when he said, I am God the Saviour, and beside me there is no other, and this faith is the joy of my heart, and my consolation forever." Vol. II, p. 256.

H. N. D.

Printed by Libri Plureos GmbH in Hamburg,
Germany